The Book On Bullies:

How To Handle Them
Without Becoming One Of Them

SUSAN K. BOYD, MS, MFT

WESTBOW
PRESS
A DIVISION OF THOMAS NELSON

Scripture marked NIV is taken from the Holy Bible, New International Version®. Copyright © 1973, 1978, 1984 Biblica. Used by permission of Zondervan. All rights reserved.

Scritpure marked RSV is taken from Revised Standard Version of the Bible, copyright 1952 [2nd edition, 1971] by the Division of Christian Education of the National Council of the Churches of Christ in the United States of America. Used by permission. All rights reserved.

WestBow Press books may be ordered through booksellers or by contacting:

WestBow Press
A Division of Thomas Nelson
1663 Liberty Drive
Bloomington, IN 47403
www.westbowpress.com
1-(866) 928-1240

Because of the dynamic nature of the Internet, any web addresses or links contained in this book may have changed since publication and may no longer be valid. The views expressed in this work are solely those of the author and do not necessarily reflect the views of the publisher, and the publisher hereby disclaims any responsibility for them.

Any people depicted in stock imagery provided by Thinkstock are models, and such images are being used for illustrative purposes only.

Certain stock imagery © Thinkstock.
All photographs and poems inside of book copyright © 2012 Susan K. Boyd

ISBN: 978-1-4497-4301-7 (e)
ISBN: 978-1-4497-4302-4 (sc)
ISBN: 978-1-4497-4303-1 (hc)

Library of Congress Control Number: 2012904663

Printed in the United States of America

WestBow Press rev. date: 04/05/2012

This book is dedicated to . . .

My husband, Jerry, who always encouraged me in my writing. I have been married to him for over forty-three years and have loved him even longer.

Jerry, I have always appreciated your strength and kindness. Thanks for being the farthest thing from a bully anyone could be.

Contents

Acknowledgments

I want to thank all my friends for asking me through the years, "So, when are you going to write a book?" They showed up at seminars I gave and asked for poems or handouts I had written so they could share them with others. I have been blessed beyond belief by the sweetness and enthusiasm of cherished friends.

I owe a debt of thanks to Dave Castro for all of his help in offering to edit and be the first person to read the rough draft. I now know why it is called a rough draft! I am grateful for his expertise, feedback, perspective, and dedication as a teacher. I know he has a real heart for this subject and for the children he helps every day.

Jeremy Weddle at WestBow Press took time to help me decide upon a subject close to his own heart. He explained there were many books about bullying on the market, but few were specifically written from a Christian perspective. I am sure there will be many more. I would be thrilled to know this little book was part of that beginning.

Maggie Webb-Conard, my Check-in Coordinator was invaluable in all the ways she helped me take this manuscript to book form. She has the patience of Job answering questions and finding solutions. Her positive attitude in working through problems is impressive.

I am thankful for the help of David Dunn and the editing department at WestBow Press for correcting my poor punctuation. They assisted me in my charts so these tools would be useful to people.

I am grateful to the helpful and patient staff at the Apple Store on Higuera Street, San Luis Obispo, California. They were lifesavers for this book and for me.

I appreciate my husband's support and insight. He listened as I read chapters to him, prompted me to write, and always believed in me.

I owe a huge acknowledgment to Florence Ellen Hoffman McClusky, my mom, who died over thirty years ago. She was an amazing woman. Over her lifetime, she was a wife, mother, nurse (during WW II), teacher, and bookkeeper. She had a strong sense of right and wrong, loved God and her family and said all she ever wanted me to do was write.

My last and most important acknowledgment is to my Lord, Jesus, who wrote his name on my heart so I would have something to write about . . .

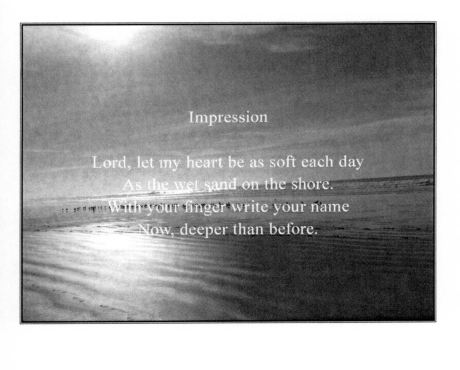

Impression

Lord, let my heart be as soft each day
As the wet sand on the shore.
With your finger write your name
Now, deeper than before.

Foreword

Is there anything worse than a bully? Bullies can steal away happy childhoods and make school a minefield to navigate. If the predator is in your own family, then home becomes an internment camp. The good news is that you graduate from school and leave home, so at last you are free of the abuser—or are you? You start a career, and guess who is the supervisor or colleague? It is someone strangely familiar—the bully.

The worst part of the bully scenario is that all the unfinished business from the past emotionally loads the present experience. We are reacting not just to what is being done to us today but to all that was done before. We may even believe the bullies' propaganda: that by speaking up or confronting them, we'll only make things worse. This belief system keeps victims in their place. They remain fodder for bullies.

On the other hand, bullies are also victims. They may have been bullied themselves as children and fear the world is divided into two groups: victims and bullies. Determined to never be victims again, they pick on anyone smaller or weaker, which gives them the reassurance they are powerful and invulnerable.

Not every victim or bully has the above-mentioned background. Some people are born introverts and can be more passive or reserved than others. That passivity, viewed as weakness, can make them targets for abusive people.

Along the same line, not all bullies had abusive childhoods. There are those who were overindulged as children and never learned there were consequences to their actions. And still others were born with impulsive and aggressive tendencies. Whatever the reasons, there is a mind-set for victims and a mind-set for bullies. Changing that mind-set is the goal of this book.

As a therapist and a Christian, I decided there needed to be a practical handbook to enable people to live values as Christ directed: "You have heard that it was said to love your neighbor and hate your enemy. But I say to you: Love your enemies and pray for those who persecute you" (Matthew 5:43-44 NIV). This book is being written to help everyone, not just Christians, if they or their family members are targets of bullying.

As long as society sees meekness as weakness and so many of the reality TV programs and movies glorify quarrelsome, aggressive personalities, Christian ethics will not necessarily be held in high esteem. Demonstrating Christ's love for the abusive and abrasive while still standing up for what is right is a tough balancing act.

How can people act and not merely react? Answering that question is the purpose of this book. A natural response to being bullied is to pray; to avoid the bullies who terrorize, hoping it will be over soon; or fight back with like tactics.

However, Scripture gives us an insight into fighting back: "For though we live in the world, we do not wage war as the world does. The weapons we fight with are not the weapons of the world. On the contrary, they have divine power to demolish strongholds. We demolish arguments and every pretense that sets itself up against the knowledge of God and we take captive every thought to make it obedient to Christ" (2 Corinthians 10:3-5 NIV). The war is on the inside as much as on the outside.

The intention of this book is to give concrete biblical strategies to empower people to know when and how finally to take action. Fortunately, the Bible is rich in true stories of heroes under fire who took control of their lives and the lives of others who suffered under the tyranny of bullies.

We have a mandate always to love and pray for enemies. However, today we are going to determine when it is time to turn the other cheek and when it is time to turn the tables.

Introduction

Bully
Definition:
*A blustering, quarrelsome, overbearing person,
who habitually badgers and intimidates smaller
or weaker people.*
(Dictionary.com)

The Bully Checklists

The following lists are itemized for easy reference. Use them as guides to equip and help you when bullying takes place in your life.

The Bullies' Mind's Eye

- ☑ Sees you at fault—you are an irritant that provokes them by just being in their world.

- ☑ Sees you as a potential threat to their domain.

- ☑ Sees you as weak and helpless-an irresistible target—wet cement they cannot pass by without leaving their footprints.

- ☑ Sees you as a testing ground for their power. How far can they go before being stopped?

- ☑ Sees you as a handy opportunity to get the attention and following of others.

The Bullies' Motivation

☑   Desire to dominate

☑   Need for control

Emotional and Physical Effects of Being Bullied
(Check boxes of symptoms experienced)

☐ Distorted self-image: "There must be something wrong with me because I'm the one singled out to be bullied."

☐ Flood of emotion, terror in particular

☐ Anxiety attacks

☐ Depression

☐ Difficulty trusting others or feeling safe

☐ Withdrawal, isolation, and avoidance behavior: doesn't want to go to school or work

☐ Imploding: self-injury, alcoholism, drug abuse, and illnesses such as high blood pressure, migraines, ulcers, irritable bowel syndrome, and others. Children who were potty trained begin to soil underwear again.

- ☐ Exploding: irritability leading to outbursts or violent behavior

- ☐ Growing pessimism and a sense of impending doom

- ☐ Difficulty concentrating on work or academics

- ☐ Interruption of sleep pattern or difficulty going to sleep.

- ☐ Hypervigilance: extreme watchfulness and monitoring of surroundings

- ☐ Startle reflex: jumps or becomes nervous at loud noises or quick movements

- ☐ Suicidal or homicidal ideation and/or behaviors

How Christ Handled Bullies

☑ Forgave the bullies but did not trust them

☑ Kept his distance when in danger

☑ Concentrated on his own goals: salvation of souls

☑ Refused to give them status

☑ Stood up for others who were bullied

☑ Avoided traps

☑ Never assumed the victim role (Note: By his own volition, he allowed himself to be crucified for others' sins but only at a certain appointed time). He was the victor, not the victim.

Practical Ways to Handle the Bullies in Your Life

BREAK FREE METHOD

☑ *B*e bold, not timid.

☑ *R*ecognize your strengths.

☑ *E*mpower yourself; find and use your voice.

☑ *A*void traps.

☑ *K*eep your distance.

☑ *F*orgive bullies; don't trust bullies.

☑ *R*efuse to be intimidated.

☑ *E*nlist help and support.

☑ *E*valuate your life goals and live them.

We will meet three different types of bullies in the first three chapters of Part I. The last three chapters in Part II will be aimed specifically at helping your children. Consider how you will use the strategies in the Break Free Method to handle the bullies in your life and the lives of those in your family.

The
'I Wills'

Today, I *will* remember
My heavenly Father is King.
I *will* hold my head up high,
Unashamed of anything.

I was petrified at times.
My heart was filled with dread.
My bully and stalker tormented me.
I hated the day ahead.

But today, I *will* put on my armor
Of God's Word, prayer, and pride,
Of having the love of my Savior
Encouraging me inside.

I *will* do whatever I must
To be safe when bullies are near.
I *won't* listen to lies or believe their disguise.
I *will* live my life without fear.

Introduction

My Personal Checklist
to Stop the Bullying
(Check only those that apply)

"I am willing to . . ."

☐ read *The Book on Bullies,*

☐ share this book with someone who is being bullied,

☐ share this book with a bully,

☐ agree that no one deserves to be bullied for any reason,

☐ pray for someone who is being bullied,

☐ pray for someone I recognize as a bully,

☐ pray God will use this book to empower me when faced with bullies,

☐ talk to my family, school, or church about what I am learning from *The Book on Bullies.*

My Plan of Action

_____

_____

_____

_____

_____

_____

_____

_____

_____

_____

_____

_____

_____

_____

_____

_____

_____

_____

_____

_____

_____

_____

_____

_____

_____

PART I

Types of Bullies

Narcissistic Bullies

Crowd Pleaser Bullies

Backdoor Bullies

CHAPTER 1

Narcissistic Bullies

A narcissist is someone who is self-absorbed and self-centered. The phrase, "It's all about me," describes this kind of person to a tee. These people need to be admired even more than they need to be liked. They can appear to be very generous or charming, but there is usually an agenda underneath this facade. The charm is reserved for people they are trying to impress. If you are not one of *those* people, you may see the other face of narcissism.

Narcissists change faces if they believe they are not getting enough respect. They can quickly get into a rage or tirade that could go on for minutes or hours. This is because at the core of their personalities lies deep shame. The shame is hidden by layers of illusions that serve to make them feel important.

The Book on Bullies:
How to Handle Them without Becoming One of Them

Being right is extremely important to narcissists. They will find a way to let others know their opinions. They also have very little tolerance for those who disagree with them. These people like to have power and to have powerful or influential friends and associates (imaginary or otherwise), money, and status. Status by association is crucial.

When narcissists come into my office for therapy for the first time, they typically look over my framed diplomas and certificates. They then question me condescendingly about whether I have enough expertise to treat them. However, once they hear me interviewed on television or the radio, I have suddenly earned my right to be their therapist and they will proudly announce our association to others.

Narcissists also have difficulty with relating personally to the pain of other people. They can occasionally feel sympathy. Feeling empathy, however, is like asking them to immediately speak a foreign language. They don't know what you are talking about.

When narcissists become bullies, they feel an all-consuming need to make you show them the respect and give them the homage they *know* they are entitled to. Entitlement is their middle name. If they don't believe they are getting respect, they will make you pay. Celebrities and famous athletes who get into the news for abusing spouses, former employees, or the hotel housekeeper are good examples of narcissistic bullies.

There are a variety of settings in which you will find narcissistic bullies. Your narcissists are coworkers in the workplace, manipulating a situation to get all the credit for the project on which everyone worked. These individuals will belittle you and argue with you in front of others or corner you if you ever disagree with them.

Children do this in the school yard, cafeteria, and, most often, the restroom, where adults can't see them. These kids brag and push other kids around. They may do this physically or by making fun of classmates.

While putting others down, they will lie about their own achievements. They will exaggerate details about grand vacations and electronic toys they have or will soon receive. Bullies also tell shocking, often fabricated stories to get attention. They become very angry if other kids challenge them about the truth of the details in their stories.

Narcissistic bullies can be found anywhere in high schools. Some examples would be star athletes or cheerleaders. However, they don't inspire and encourage people as others on their teams or squads may do. Instead, they use their power to make fun of others they believe are making the team look bad. They don't necessarily care about the people they lead; they just want the lead.

Narcissistic bullies also harass and devalue more marginal students. They will use any means to stay on top. Taylor Swift sang her song, "Mean," to these individuals: "Someday I'll be living in a big old city. And all you're ever gonna be is mean. Someday I'll be big enough so you can't hit me. And all you're ever gonna be is mean. Why you gotta be so mean?"

One of the best examples in the Bible of a narcissistic bully may be King Saul. His story can be found in I Samuel. He *appeared* to be a humble man in the beginning. Wasn't he hiding in the baggage area before his coronation? Remember, at the core of a narcissist's personality is a fear of shame (1 Samuel 10: 21-24).

He did well as king for a while, until faced with a bully named Goliath (1 Samuel 17-18). Saul and all his soldiers were afraid to face the huge Philistine. A young shepherd boy, David, bringing supplies to his older brothers on the front line, couldn't understand why no one stood up to this bully.

Saul gave David his armor and sword. These things were too big and heavy, and so David set them aside. Then the shepherd boy slew Goliath with nothing but an early version of a slingshot and a well-placed rock. Saul and his soldiers, inspired, then raced across enemy lines and defeated the Philistines.

After that, Saul and David became close. Well, they were as close as someone can ever really be to a narcissist. Remember, narcissists like having famous friends or associates. That is, as long as the narcissists continue to look good. David became one of the leading captains in Saul's army. He was a hero to Saul and to all his people.

One fateful day, David returned victorious from a battle to an adoring crowd that cheered, "Saul has slain his thousands and David his ten thousands." As King Saul heard this, fear and shame (remember, a narcissist has to have all the attention and respect) turned quickly to rage. He began to obsess and plot against David. So began the one-sided rivalry and vendetta of a narcissistic king turned narcissistic bully (1 Samuel 18: 5-9).

David, as a young man, was possibly the best example in the Old Testament of how to handle bullies without becoming one of them. David loved God and he loved his friend King Saul. Yet no matter how many times David showed forgiveness and kindness to Saul, nothing ever changed (1 Samuel 18-31).

You know the importance of forgiveness. Yet you must find a way to stand up for yourself without exacting revenge. You do this knowing the bully may never change, but you can't let the bully change you—even if the bully is a friend or loved one who has wounded you deeper than a stranger ever could.

Goliath was an easier adversary for David. David didn't see him as God's chosen king, nor was Goliath his mentor and trusted friend. The Sauls in our lives hurt us the most because they once acted as if they cared for us the most.

David kept true to who he was, no matter what Saul's tactics. Keep your dignity and integrity, and you will avoid becoming the bully you hate.

David, as a shepherd boy, had been summoned to play his stringed instrument for Saul to comfort him when he became agitated. However, when David came to play for the king after becoming the favorite of the people, all Saul could feel was hatred. As David played, Saul picked up his spear and tried to pin him to the wall (1 Samuel 18: 10-11).

David used most of the strategies of the Break Free Method. He knew when it was time to leave and put some distance between he and his king.

David and a band of loyal followers became hunted men. Twice, it would seem, God placed the bloodthirsty Saul into David's hands. Once was in a cave where David and his men were hiding. David took out his knife and cut off a piece of Saul's garment. David was immediately sorry for the act. Later he shouted out to Saul to look at the proof of his loyalty, that he had been that close to his enemy but did not hurt him when he had the chance.

Saul instantly—and temporarily—felt convicted of his mistreatment of his loyal young friend and told him so. David did not believe Saul's beautifully crafted speech of remorse. David knew not to trust himself to this narcissistic bully. He was right, for the manhunt resumed (1 Samuel 24: 1-22).

In another instance, David snuck into Saul's camp. He stole the water jug and spear that lay next to Saul. God had a deep sleep fall over the king and his soldiers. Instead of killing his enemy with his own spear, David, again, shouted to them to look and see that he had been that close and did Saul no harm (1 Samuel 26: 1-25).

In my counseling office I call this interaction a "Just-For-the-Record" moment. This is the time you avoid vague generalities and point out specific events and times to prove your point. This is the best form of communication when there is a dispute. Once, again, Saul proclaimed David's innocence and his own regret for the pursuit of his friend. David, wisely, did not trust him and kept his distance.

The biggest mistake that can be made with this type of bully is to be so relieved that the bullying is over and moved by the seemingly contrite apologies that you make yourself vulnerable to him or her again. David never made that mistake.

Saul was wounded in battle. He then fell on his own sword and later died. A messenger ran to report this news to David, imagining he would be elated. Instead, possibly to everyone's amazement, David mourned Saul's passing even though it meant he, himself, would become king (2 Samuel 1: 1-27).

This is such a godly trait. We are not to gloat over our enemies' bad fortune or God will be displeased. Isn't it amazing that God does not wish the worst things on even the worst people? He wants us all to repent and know we have a Savior who died for the awful sins we all commit. The narcissistic bullies may never have empathy, but we can.

David wrote many of the psalms while he was being chased, suffering at the hands of his own bully. His writings have brought comfort to people down through the ages. God had a plan for David's life. God has a plan for yours and mine. The shepherd boy became king. What will you and I become?

Making or Breaking of a Bully

Lord,
Don't let the bullies
Change the person I am.
If I take their hatred as my own
I'll never understand . . .

How to truly forgive
The way you do,
Or know the strength of mercy
That comes from you.

Show me when to take a stand
And when it is time to go.
But never let me become
The bullies that I know.

Take the bully out of me
So I'm compassionate and kind.
I'll drop my grudges in the sea,
Where they're impossible to find.

Narcissistic Bullies

My Own Personal Inventory

Do you have any narcissistic bullies in your life?

How could you use David's example to keep the narcissistic bullies from overpowering you?

What do you like about David in this chapter?

Make a list of practical strategies you can put into action when the narcissistic bullies try to hurt you.

Is there anyone you are jealous of or angry with who has become for you a David? If so, how can you keep from reacting like King Saul?

Will you pray to develop more empathy toward the David in your life?

Write a short prayer asking specifically what you would like the Lord to do for you.

My Plan of Action
for Handling Narcissistic Bullies

_____

_____

_____

_____

_____

_____

_____

_____

_____

_____

_____

_____

_____

_____

_____

_____

_____

_____

_____

_____

_____

_____

_____

_____

_____

_____

CHAPTER 2

Crowd Pleaser Bullies

There once was a bully named Saul. Only this Saul can be found in the book of Acts in the New Testament. His obsession was to round up Christians and throw them in jail. While on the road to Damascus, hot on the hunt for those Jesus-followers, he was blinded by a light. A voice said, "Saul, Saul why do you persecute me?"

Saul, confused and frightened, naturally asked, "Who are you, Lord?"

To his shock the voice proclaimed, "I am Jesus whom you are persecuting . . ." (Acts 9:4-5 RSV). That is how Saul the bully later became Paul the apostle.

Paul's heart was changed, and his message changed the world. Paul then had his own tormentors biting at his heels for the rest of his life. Yet his was a story of courage and success that no bullies could undermine, not even this group that make up our second type of bullies: The crowd pleasers.

Crowd pleasers usually, but not always, run in packs. They may form a group with similar goals, like gangs, mobs, families with cult-like traits and fanatical religious sects. Crowd pleasers will take recruits who will discredit or demean anyone who disagrees with them. "You are either with us or you are against us," could be their creed.

Imagine the bitter betrayal felt by the high priest and Sanhedrin who sent Paul to arrest Christians then discovered he had become one of them. Paul then became their target. Paul's bullies feared losing power and control. That insecurity fueled the flames of jealousy as they moved to protect their domain.

The apostle was a great example of how to take a stand and use voice in defiance of those who would malign and sabotage. He was a Pharisee, scholar, and a legal mind before he was ever a Christian. Having that background, he was equipped to state his case to the people in the synagogues and in the marketplaces.

Paul never gave up control to his enemies. When they demanded he go to trial under their laws, he demanded to be tried by Roman laws and present his case to Caesar. His calling and promise from God was that he would bring the message of salvation before kings (Acts 9:15-16).

The Book on Bullies:
How to Handle Them without Becoming One of Them

Paul used his voice and intellect to go where he wanted to go, not where his bullies allowed him to go. If crowd pleasers can keep you quiet, then the only voice the crowd ever hears is theirs.

Just as important as speaking up is the lesson Paul taught us about keeping our world large.

Paul's world was never small. (Note: Even when Paul was in prison and unable to visit churches he established, he was writing letters to encourage them.) No bully would intimidate him into staying in a corner.

Paul kept his eye on the goal. God said Paul would take his message to the Gentiles. If the bullies were going to catch Paul, they would have to find him first because he was always moving. He traveled to Asia, Greece, Galatia, and anywhere God pointed his finger.

Paul didn't waste time looking for his adversaries. He was too busy doing God's work. They would have to look for him. People who have been abused often try to stay away from places they know their bullies frequent. This is wise unless those bullied become controlled by their own fear. Their fear begins to generalize to include places their bullies *might* start going. I encourage the people I counsel to choose where they want to go and not let their world get smaller while the bullies' world gets bigger.

The Book on Bullies:
How to Handle Them without Becoming One of Them

I also recommend that clients who have been bullied take a friend with them when they go out into the world. Paul had companions who traveled with him evangelizing and checking on the churches so they would not feel alone either. We need to stay in relationships, not retreat into isolation. Keep your world big and take trusted people along with you.

Paul demonstrated how to handle the bullying crowd pleasers. The best example may have been from his mission trip in Philippi (Acts 16). He and Silas were preaching in the town square. Paul cast a demon out of a woman. She was a slave working for the local merchants. She brought in revenue for them by telling people's fortunes.

Once the demon was gone, so was her ability to tell fortunes and make money for her owners. The merchants incited the crowds against Paul and Silas. The two men were severely flogged, put into stocks, and thrown into prison.

It would seem the bullies had won. The two evangelists, however, sang hymns as the jailer and prisoners listened through the night. Suddenly, an earthquake shook the city and the prison doors broke open. The jailer feared for his own life if his prisoners were missing. The apostles called out to him, reassuring their jailer they were all still there.

The Book on Bullies:
How to Handle Them without Becoming One of Them

The jailer took Paul and Silas to his home that night and he and his whole household became converts to Christianity. Paul and Silas returned to their cell. The next morning the magistrates sent an order for their release. (Perhaps they were worried the citizens would attribute the earthquake to Paul's God!)

However, Paul turned the tables on them, saying, "They beat us publicly without a trial even though we are Roman citizens and threw us into prison. Now do they want to get rid of us that quietly? No! Let them come and escort us out."

The magistrates then came and pleaded with Paul and Silas. The authorities escorted them from the prison and begged them to please leave the city.

The bullies who were at one time crowd pleasers got the bad news from Paul. What if the Roman authorities heard about the unlawful whipping of two Roman citizens? The bullies found themselves suddenly in danger. Bullies back down when there is a strong possibility they will be punished for their behavior.

The apostles did not rush to leave the area. They had made new converts when they first arrived, such as Lydia. Soon after her conversion she opened her home as a church for the band of new believers. Paul and Silas stopped by to bless, fellowship with, and probably encourage them before leaving.

Paul stood up for Silas, himself, and for what was right in Philippi and throughout his ministry. Christians in Philippi knew, at least for a while, the bullies would think twice before targeting them.

When we stand up for ourselves we are standing up for all those watching who are afraid they will be next on the bullies' list. Who are the people watching you that need to know they can have a voice and they are not alone? When you speak up, you are not just saving yourself from the bullies who are crowd pleasers. You are probably saving others who have yet to find their voice.

A Voice

Lord, I can no longer be silent.
I take hold of your courage to speak.
If the words I say could help others today,
Then this is the promise I keep.

Crowd Pleaser Bullies

My Own Personal Inventory

Are you experiencing any bullying by a group of people like the crowd pleaser bullies?

How are these crowd pleasers trying to take control?

How are you able to stay focused on what God wants you to do instead of what the bullies want you to do?

Do you ever hear yourself belittling and demeaning other groups of people with whom you disagree?

What are you going to do or say to stand up for yourself and what you believe without ridiculing others?

My Plan of Action
for Handling Crowd Pleaser Bullies

_____

_____

_____

_____

_____

_____

_____

_____

_____

_____

_____

_____

_____

_____

_____

_____

_____

_____

_____

_____

_____

_____

CHAPTER 3

Backdoor Bullies

Not all bullies have the "in your face" approach. They don't act like the rude stranger that you know is dangerous and whom you have no intention of letting through the front door. These sneaky bullies use tactics to make you feel as comfortable as Lucy Ricardo when her friend Ethel Mertz came through the back kitchen door for a cup of coffee in an old *I Love Lucy* episode.

But unlike the relationship between the Ricardos and Mertzes, these smiling people are not your friends. They are usually passive-aggressive individuals, attacking with plenty of deniability built into their behavior. Backdoor bullies use familiarity or humor to set you at ease. Then, when all your defenses are down, they spring the trap. They begin to make remarks and do things to discredit, humiliate,

The Book on Bullies:
How to Handle Them without Becoming One of Them

and badger you. They count on no one challenging them. After all, they care about you, right?

Who are these back door bullies making themselves at home in our lives? They are the teenage cyber-bullies talking other kids into taking questionable photos and sending them to phones or computers where the anonymous bullies wait to post online.

They may also move from humorous texts to cruel teasing or harassment. The mere act of typing on a keyboard can become intoxicating to bullies who by badgering and intimidating can control someone else's emotions.

Unsupervised young children are just as much at risk. They are technologically savvy, too. They are comfortable with the Internet, open to friendships, and want to be included.

Because of that desire for inclusion, the cyber-bullies know they can use computers, social networking sites, phone texts, or e-mails as a way of exerting their power over their peers. They do this all under the radar and in complete silence.

It is not uncommon for those being bullied to become depressed or even suicidal if the bullying becomes intense and widespread. The targeted seldom tell their parents, unless asked, for fear they won't be able to continue to talk with friends on the computer or cell phone.

The Book on Bullies:
How to Handle Them without Becoming One of Them

I counsel families to keep the family computer out of kids' bedrooms and in high traffic rooms. Families need to have an understanding that parents *may, when necessary,* read e-mails or texts, and be informed before kids go on the Internet. Parents are wise to install software that keeps their kids away from dangerous websites.

Open communication about being careful and kind is a great teaching opportunity for parents. Asking whether anyone has been bullied or has seen bullying can be an enlightening family round table discussion. (This will be discussed further in chapter 4.)

Unfortunately, some families are backdoor bullies themselves. The dysfunction shows up as a disregard for personal boundaries and peoples' feelings. Ongoing snide remarks, sarcasm, or cruel humor aimed at someone's weakness moves from joking to an attack.

Bullies justify their behavior by saying, "You are just too sensitive. Toughen up," or "You know I was just kidding." Any complaining about their treatment of you will probably result in, "Now you're just being defensive," "You can't take a little kidding," or "Oh, get over it!"

Wrestling and tickling can be considered just fun sport in families until someone says he or she has had enough. Is the initiator the same person most of the time? Is this individual stronger or older? If someone bigger continues to physically control someone smaller or weaker, that is bullying.

A quick response to family bullying is the best. Here are a few proactive words that might make an impact, or at least raise awareness: "Stop!" "Knock it off," "I don't deserve that," "I don't want you to say that—or do that—to me, again," "Do you know what you just said to me?" Then repeat the name the bully called you. Ignoring bullies, however, can also work to discourage them if what they are looking for is a reaction.

Some families habitually pick on one another until they are made to quit. If bullies are not confronted, family scapegoats become conflicted. They don't know whether to pull away to safety or stay and attempt to win approval in hopes the mean behavior will stop. Respect and trust can be irreparably damaged.

The backdoor bullies on the job site or in the office may be coworkers or colleagues who alternate between acting like your friend or acting like your worst enemy. These coworkers talk behind your back. They make inside jokes about you with other coworkers. When they are with you, rather than disagree, they will roll their eyes, give big sighs, and mutter complaints about you as they turn on their heels and abruptly leave the room.

The Book on Bullies:
How to Handle Them without Becoming One of Them

The backdoor bullies use their passive-aggressive behaviors in subtle ways. Doing jobs they want to do rather than work that helps you finish joint projects is a way of hurting your work performance. Another method is being habitually late for work or suspiciously absent when the result will be overloading you with their work or making you late for deadlines.

These individuals will try to get into your personal life and business. You may mistake this for genuine interest. They seem friendly, but in actuality you just become more vulnerable to them.

Coworkers who act as backdoor bullies will pull you into inner-office conflict. They will bate you with questions about your boss or other coworkers. They act sincere, as if they value your advice. They will save your comment for an opportunity to quote you to others.

Before long, whenever these coworkers ask questions, you think of all the ways they could twist your words before you answer. You become confused and frustrated, wishing you had never confided in them and that you could get your autonomy back.

The best way to handle bullies is to stay focused on your work. Refuse to answer or talk about anyone. (Note: This is a good communication principle that works in family and school settings as well.)

The Book on Bullies:
How to Handle Them without Becoming One of Them

They tell you they want to know what you think about a problem they are having with others. Stay out of the middle with comments like: "Sorry, I really can't help you with that," "Sounds like something you need to talk to them about," "I don't know enough about it to comment," "I have to get my work done." Then get to work. This is a workplace, and the only way to stay out of the drama is to get off their stage.

Employers or supervisors operating as backdoor bullies believe they are your mentors, but are duplicitous and contradictory. They make and change rules on a whim so you are not sure what rule you are breaking. You are given a job, then taken off of it before you can finish and assigned to a different task. Then you are criticized for not completing the first job satisfactorily.

These supervisors or employers act as if they are the victims. They believe they are being undermined, which is how they justify their abusive behavior. They communicate their frustration, much of the time indirectly. They will shake their heads, throw up their hands, and grumble their disapproval: "I guess I am the only one who cares about getting things done right." Swearing about you rather than at you is not uncommon.

The "close the door and come into my office" job performance review can be a nightmare unless you know how to confront the bullying. Character assassination is bullying. These bullies will use big generalities and derogatory labels to attack you. An example would be an employer who rants that he or she has done everything for you and yet, "You are lazy and make stupid decisions."

In these situations, be direct and request an example so you both are looking at the same behavior. "Could you be more specific? When, exactly, did you see me being lazy or making a stupid decision?"

If you are accused in vague generalities like, "You just don't care about your work. You aren't a team player," reply with, "It *is* important to me to do a good job. So please tell me a situation or a time and place you saw that happening."

You may never back a bullying boss down, but you can back him or her up. Listen and learn from the constructive part of the criticism and always agree with truth. If you need to apologize, do it sincerely but without appearing or sounding smaller or weaker, as that is inevitably what bullies look for and pick on in others. Direct the conversation to narrow and specific examples.

These backdoor bullies will also make you indebted to them if possible, which ensnares you. How can you feel comfortable confronting someone to whom you owe so much? This ensures their control over you. They may frequently buy you lunches, give you special privileges, gifts, and loans one moment, and make very personal comments about you the next. They may also disrespect your personal space and rights; an example of this behavior is sexual harassment, which often goes unreported. Don't be manipulated. Be aware of the bullies' tactics and tricks.

Jesus had his share of backdoor bullies circling and stalking his ministry. They were the religious leaders called the Pharisees. As his popularity increased, his enemies became more jealous and worried about losing their influence in his shadow. Because Jesus was held in high esteem by so many, the Pharisees had to use the backdoor method to trap and defame him. Of course this technique was full of insincere adoration coupled with devious questions.

Probably the most well known trick question ever given Jesus was whether the occupied Jews were to pay tribute to the Romans, their enemies. The Pharisees came in the back door like great admirers and posed the question. If Jesus said it was wrong to pay taxes to their enemies, he would surely have been arrested. If he told them they should pay taxes, he would have lost all credibility with his own people.

"Teacher, we know that you are true, and teach the way of God truthfully; and care for no man, for you do not regard the position of men." (Trying to get in the back door with flattery, the Pharisees laid the trap.) "Tell us what you think, is it lawful to pay taxes to Caesar or not" (Matthew 22:16-17 RSV)?

Jesus kept fast to *his* goal of leading people to eternal life and eternal things. He took every devious plot of his bullies and turned it into a moment of decision for his listeners. He never let the bullies get him off track.

Jesus, aware of their malice, said, "Why do you put me to the test, you hypocrites? Show me the money for the tax." And they brought him a coin and Jesus said to them, "Whose likeness and inscription is this?"

They said, "Caesar's."

Then he said to them, "Render, therefore, to Caesar the things that are Caesar's and to God the things that are God's." When they heard this, they marveled, and they left him and went their way (Matthew 22: 18-22 RSV).

Jesus knew that, at an appointed time set by his heavenly father, he would go to the cross. He also knew his bullies would take him there. He had much to do before then. He taught and fellowshipped. He healed the sick and freed people from demons, sorrow, and discouragement. Jesus focused his attention where *he wanted it,* not where the bullies wanted it.

The Book on Bullies:
How to Handle Them without Becoming One of Them

There were days, of course, when Jesus stayed away from Jerusalem because he knew the bullies were lying in wait. He surrounded himself with his twelve disciples and many others for whom we do not even have names. These are prudent measures to take, then and now, for anyone plagued by bullies.

Jesus, however, was not afraid of his attackers but chose his own time to be arrested. He confronted the Pharisees when he had to, because bullies don't stop until they are made to stop.

Yet Jesus' calling was to die for the bullies. As he hung on the cross, they taunted him. He did not answer them back but remembered why he was there. Looking to heaven he called out on their behalf—and ours—"Father, forgive them, for they know not what they do."

Jesus was no one's doormat, but he was my salvation. I have been his bully. Every time I carelessly sinned, I held the spike and drove it through him with every justification I used. My sin, not just the Pharisees', gave him his scars. He forgave me, too, that day at the cross. He forgave you as well. All who love Christ will be whole in heaven, without blemish or imperfection. Only Jesus will bear the marks of all the bullies in this world on his body for eternity.

Scars

Lord,
I am sorry for all the bullying.
You forgave me at such a cost.
I pushed thorns in your brow
And nailed you to a cross.

When I see you in heaven, Lord,
I'll cry when I hold your hand.
I'll know for eternity you have that scar
Because of who I am.

"Oh, child, I don't wear these scars
To show what you did or where you've been.
Don't you know? It's because I have these scars
That today you have no sin."

Backdoor Bullies

My Own Personal Inventory

Have you ever known someone who acted like a friend but who continually hurt your feelings or criticized you?

How do you speak up for yourself when someone puts you down?

List some statements you can make or actions you can take to stand up for yourself.

My Plan of Action
to Handle Backdoor Bullies

_____

_____

_____

_____

_____

_____

_____

_____

_____

_____

_____

_____

_____

_____

_____

_____

_____

_____

_____

_____

_____

_____

_____

PART II

Ways to Help Your Children

Be Bullyproof

Become Someone Who Won't Bully

Be a Bystander No More

CHAPTER 4

Be Bullyproof

Being bullied or picked on is part of growing up. Kids just have to learn to deal with it. Have you heard that? Is it true? Let's look at what we do know is true.

According to the report, *Indicators of School Crime and Safety: 2008*, by the National Center for Educational Statistics, about 32 percent of children reported being bullied at school. Of those students, 79 percent reported being bullied inside the school building, 23 percent reported being bullied on school grounds, and 4 percent reported being cyber-bullied.[1]

The 2001 National Crime Victimization Survey, by the US Department of Education, found that there were no major differences between private and public schools or between the number of girls and boys being bullied. They discovered bullied kids were more likely to get into fights and to take a weapon to school for protection from their peers. Bullied children were also more likely to receive lower grades than those students who were not being bullied, according to their research.[2]

The Department of Education website points out that bullied students are more at risk for anxiety and depression, health problems, and mental health problems.[3]

Researchers in Virginia found that school-wide passing rates on three different standardized exams were three to six times lower in schools where bullying was pervasive. It was concluded that children are less able to concentrate on learning if they are afraid of ongoing bullying at school.[4]

A study published in the American Journal of Psychiatry suggested that victims of bullying may be more than twice as likely to develop psychotic symptoms (such as delusions or paranoia) as compared to kids who aren't abused by their peers.[5]

According to "Stop Bullying," an article on the stopbullying.gov website, children who suffer at the hands of bullies have increased suicidal thoughts and tendencies persisting into adulthood. Being bullied was associated with their health status as much as three years later. The habitually bullied are more likely to retaliate with extreme violent measures. Out of the fifteen school shooting cases in the 1990s, twelve of the shooters had a history of being bullied.[6]

So maybe bullying is not as harmless as we once thought. What, then, can parents do to bullyproof their kids? First, understand they will probably not tell you it is happening. So you can help them by having a family roundtable discussion about what bullying is. Start with very general questions.

Ask if they have seen bullying at their school, in the neighborhood, or anywhere else. Have them write or make up a definition of bullying. Afterwards, share the definition from the Introduction of this book.

Then suggest each child or teenager in the family make a list of words or names bullies call someone. Have everyone in the family write out or share all the things bullies do to scare, embarrass, or hurt people. Ask them what they think would be worse. Children and teenagers want to share with their parents when they are afraid or in trouble. They just don't want to be in more trouble by telling.

Your children may share as the questions become more personal: "Have you ever been bullied by anyone, even someone you might consider as a friend?"

People feel relieved to lay down a burden they have been carrying around like an invisible weight. If they appear sad or uncomfortable, they may need some reassurance. Remind them that no one ever deserves to be bullied for any reason.

Once you suspect your children are victims of bullying, look at the checklist in the Introduction section under Emotional and Physical Effects of Being Bullied. Note any symptoms your children display.

Kids won't always share when they are being intimidated or pushed around by others. If you believe your children are being bullied, ask their friends' parents to check with their children about bullying at school or in the neighborhood. Talk to your children's teachers and ask them to keep an eye out for the bullying you suspect.

If your children or teenagers tell you they are being bullied, talk to them about the Break Free Method Checklist found in the Introduction. Below is a specific plan of action you also can encourage them to take:

1. Walk away and ignore the bullies.
2. Have friends go with you to tell a teacher or trusted adult.
3. Stay with friends. There is more safety in numbers.
4. Use your voice and tell the bullies firmly, "Stop it!"

5. Avoid bullying back. This only escalates the situation and may get you suspended instead of the bully.
6. Keep doing what you enjoy doing—don't give attention to the bullies.[7]

If bullying is ongoing, you have the right as a parent of a student to talk directly to the principal and ask what is being done to ensure school safety. Getting the school involved in an anti-bullying movement with outside speakers and group discussions in class settings each year can rally peer pressure against bullying. This is the most potent antidote to bullying on school grounds yet.

If bullies are in the neighborhood, talk to the other parents to be on alert. Tell the parents of the bullies when it is witnessed. Encouraging your children and teenagers to choose friends who treat them with respect and consideration helps them know they don't have to take abuse to keep a friend.

Church youth groups need to integrate Bible studies and Good Samaritan type programs that give kids a chance to share and develop strategies to stop the bullying. Challenging youth to do something kind everyday will keep them from becoming bullies. Encouraging them to stand with someone else who is being victimized or

The Book on Bullies:
How to Handle Them without Becoming One of Them

to go with them to tell an adult are good ways to build character.

A productive way of discussing bullying as a family is to have a weekly Bible study together. Do a character study on heroes of the Bible as they handle bullies using the Break Free Method discussed in my Introduction.

One of the most compelling life stories in the Bible on this subject is Joseph. It is told in the book of Genesis (Genesis 37, 39-50). Bullied and sold into slavery by his own brothers, falsely accused by his master's wife in Egypt and thrown into prison for years, Joseph focused on pleasing God and doing his best wherever he happened to be. God eventually elevated him to the most powerful position in Egypt next only to Pharaoh.

Anyone who has ever suffered at the hands of bullies can't help but relish the climax to the story. The brothers, years later, came to Egypt for food. They had to come to the powerful Joseph who handled the grain distribution throughout the country. They didn't recognize him, but he recognized them.

Joseph tested their character to see if they had changed and made his former bullies squirm. It was then that they realized how it felt to be trapped and helpless under someone else's control.

The difference between Joseph and his brothers was that Joseph put them in a tight spot mainly to see if they really had changed and if they were caring for his little brother Benjamin. The exciting ending of the story shows Joseph's maturity in the Lord through the years of imprisonment and prominence.

As Joseph revealed his identity in Genesis 45 he embraced his onetime bullies with tears and forgiveness. He praised God for what his creator had been doing all those years behind the scenes.

"I am your brother, Joseph, whom you sold into Egypt. And now do not be distressed or angry with yourselves, because you sold me here; for God sent me before you to preserve life. For the famine has been in the land these two years; and there are yet five years in which there will be neither plowing nor harvest. And God sent me before you to preserve for you a remnant on earth, and to keep alive for you many survivors. So it was not you who sent me here but God and he has made me a father to Pharaoh and lord of all his house and ruler over all the land of Egypt" (Genesis 45:4-8 RSV).

Over the years I have counseled many people who have carried emotional scars of being bullied, having never told a soul until they entered my office. And their suffering is heartbreaking. Even worse is the bitterness and mistrust that can change a person so that he or she is angrier than the ones who perpetrated the abuse. Joseph never let that happen to him. Because he refused to let the bullies have the last word concerning his life, he was greatly used and promoted by his God.

Give your children the opportunity to share what they may have been hiding from you out of fear the bullying will intensify once you know. Then share with them the hope Joseph and others in Scripture offer.

The bullies don't have to win. "As for you, you meant evil against me; but God meant it for good, to bring it about that many people should be kept alive as they are today" (Genesis 50:20 RSV).

Story's End

Sadly it often seems
The villains win out.
They are malicious and cunning,
They proudly strut about.

Faithful Joseph in prison
Kept in step with his Father above.
In God's time he came to power
And ruled with love.

Be Bullyproof

My Own Personal Inventory

No one ever deserves to be bullied. If you are being bullied what two people would you feel safe enough to talk to about it.

Name three ways you might be able to get the upper hand with a bully (like Joseph did when his brothers came to Egypt) without becoming a bully yourself?

Read more details of the story of Joseph in Genesis 37 and 39-50. What do you appreciate about Joseph's character?

How do you like the way Joseph handled the bullies in his life?

Do you think it was hard for Joseph not to want revenge on his brothers? What kept him from paying them back for all the pain they caused him in his life?

My Plan of Action
to Be Bullyproof

_____

_____

_____

_____

_____

_____

_____

_____

_____

_____

_____

_____

_____

_____

_____

_____

_____

_____

_____

_____

_____

_____

_____

_____

_____

CHAPTER 5

Become Someone Who Won't Bully

According to the American Academy of Pediatrics, the best way to prevent aggressive behavior is to give your child a stable, secure home life with firm, loving discipline and full-time supervision during the toddler and preschool years.[1] This information is very true. As a family therapist I would also include the importance of consistent and fair non-reactive discipline throughout childhood. Children learn what they live even more than what they are told.

If parents are fighting, overbearing, violent, or neglectful, children will follow suit. Children learn their problem-solving skills from their surroundings. How to handle conflict is learned from listening and watching parents more than all the lectures children might receive.

The Book on Bullies:
How to Handle Them without Becoming One of Them

Moms or dads may not realize how much they reinforce bullying behavior by their own language and labels. "He's just a mean kid!" "Just keep out of his way," "She's a tough little girl," "We all know not to cross her," "You deserve what you get if you aggravate him," "Oh, that's just the way my kids are."

Sometimes, loving, high functioning parents have children or teenagers who struggle with Attention Deficit Hyperactivity Disorder or even the early onset of a Bipolar Disorder. These can be great kids, but handling their impulsivity and angry outbursts is like trying to hold onto water. Impulse control can help reduce the likelihood they will bully.

The biggest favor you can give these children is to teach them to ask themselves before they do something rash, "What are three possible consequences if I do this?" They can train themselves to slow down and reason cause and result before they act.

Some children are overindulged and seldom given limits. They will roll right over someone else to get what they want. They have not heard or learned the word "No" and can become outraged if they don't get instant gratification. Typically these are also kids that have not been taught to consider another's feelings. They can easily become bullies.

The Book on Bullies:
How to Handle Them without Becoming One of Them

A solution to help the overindulged kids is for parents to examine their own motives for giving in so easily to their children's whims. Trying to buy affection or avoid conflict by *not* saying no are problems parents need to solve within and between themselves. Moms and dads need to quit apologizing for saying no. If you are that parent, this does not mean saying no as a knee jerk reaction. However, when you do need to say it, mean it. And hold to it.

Because you are reading this book and this section, you are obviously a concerned parent wanting to help your children be kind to others. You may not fall into the above categories. So you don't quite know why your children are bullying. You might not get a complete answer, but for insight you can always ask them, "Why do you think you did that?" Bullying needs to be addressed for their sake as much as for those they bully.

Children who bully are, themselves, in danger of long-term consequences. Bullies engage early in sexual activity and are more apt to have traffic citations and criminal convictions. In one study, 60 percent of boys who bullied others in middle school had a criminal conviction by the age of twenty-four. They are also much more likely to abuse romantic partners, spouses, and children as adults.[2]

The Book on Bullies:
How to Handle Them without Becoming One of Them

Look at the checklist for indicators your children may be bullying. (Check the boxes where applicable)

- ☐ Unaccounted-for "loot" they say others traded or gave them
- ☐ Unaccounted-for money in backpacks
- ☐ Bragging behavior and mean-spirited play
- ☐ Aggressive behavior in the neighborhood, home, or school
- ☐ Animals trembling or hiding when they enter a room
- ☐ Expression of joy when they hurt others
- ☐ Poor social skills
- ☐ Obsession with popularity

The more indicators checked, the higher the likelihood of bullying.

Let's solve the problem so that these kids can have satisfying relationships and be people others look forward to being with instead of dreading. The first step is not to be gullible. If you see the indicators, check them out.

Once you have the proof, begin enforcing consequences like requiring them to do work for others without pay. Most importantly, they need to make the wrong right. They have to give items back. Take your children to the home of their victims and stand with them as they apologize.

Changing the bullies' mindset comes sometimes only after the behavior changes. Teach them that saying "I am sorry" can make a difference and possibly get friends back. Reassure them that as they try harder to be kinder, their resolve will pay off.

Explain to them that the Bible describes repentance simply as the chance to turn around and go a different way. Assure them that God forgives them if they confess their sins to him as he forgives you when you confess yours. Suggest they get alone with God and ask him to help them go in a better direction.

Teaching your children basic anger management skills can also help them, not only today but throughout their lives. Here are the three "Bs" that I give my clients who struggle with bullying:

1. *Breathe* deeply in through the nose and hold it for eight seconds, then slowly blow out like a whistle until there is no more breath. Repeat several times. This calms both anxiety and anger.
2. *Break* the tension by taking a time out and walking away to cool down.

3. *Be in control,* not out of control—start controlling self, stop trying to control others.

Your next step as a parent is to nurture empathy in your children. This is something that has gotten lost in their lives while they were bullying.

My favorite professor in my graduate program in Marriage & Family Counseling was Dr. Chuck Wall. He was inspirational. He is best known around the world for the phrase he coined and with which he challenged his students: "Today, go out into the community and commit one random, senseless act of kindness."[3]

I remember years later watching Morgan Freeman playing God in the wonderful movie *Evan Almighty.* The movie ended with Dr. Wall's quote. What a difference that one simple phrase has had on the world and the people who picked up the challenge!

One way to spark interest in helping others might be to have your children pick out a journal and tell them to make a list of "senseless, random acts of kindness" they could do in a month. Then challenge them to follow through and write the date they accomplish each act. Praise them when they share their journal entries with you.

Another avenue for helping your children find their empathy is to focus on helping other children. Before the holidays, many churches participate in the Christmas Child Good Samaritan's Purse Shoebox Ministry. You might go with your kids and shop for items for a boy or girl and pack them in a shoebox. The gift boxes are collected at various churches and sent to children who would have no Christmas gift otherwise. (See Samaritanspurse.org/occ for more information.)

If you decide to do a project like the Shoebox Ministry, concentrate on getting your children directly involved. For instance, let them pick the toys for the box and put them into the cart and onto the conveyor belt at the register. Ask them to choose the wrapping paper to decorate the box. They need to make the decisions and do the work. *Empathy is developed when there is an emotional connection and investment in caring how someone else is affected.*

Visiting children's shelters or convalescent homes with your children can help them reach out to people who need their visits. Your children may feel uncomfortable at first, but encourage them that they are making a difference in someone's life. Take cookies that you baked together.

Children don't always know how good helping others can make them feel until they do it. The actions can precede the feelings. Keep all these trips short so you build positive memories that hopefully turn into a lifestyle.

The Book on Bullies:
How to Handle Them without Becoming One of Them

The good news about guiding children away from bullying is that they are going to be happier, healthier people emotionally and interpersonally. They need to believe that they are better than their behavior. If they show more compassion in the future, their past instances of bullying need not define who they are.

Remember some of the most wonderful Bible heroes fell into bullying when they were not staying close to the Lord and his Word. It was also the saddest time of their lives.

King David, who led such a stellar life as a young man, later committed adultery with a woman named Bathsheba. She became pregnant with David's child. She was the wife of one of David's most loyal soldiers. David plotted and had her husband, Uriah, a righteous man, killed on the front lines of battle. Then David took her to the palace to be his own wife (2 Samuel 11). Nathan, God's prophet, entered the palace and made a troubling report to the king.

"There were two men in a certain town, one rich and the other poor. The rich man had a very large number of sheep and cattle, but the poor man had nothing except one poor little ewe lamb he had bought. He raised it, and it grew up with him and his children. It shared his food, drank from his cup, and even slept in his arms. It was like a daughter to him. Now a traveler came to the rich man, but the rich man refrained from taking one of his own sheep or cattle to prepare a meal for the traveler who had come to him. Instead, he took the ewe lamb that belonged to the poor man and prepared it for the one who had come to him" (2 Samuel 12:1-4 NIV).

David burned with anger against the man and said to Nathan, "As sure as the Lord lives, the man who did this deserves to die! He must pay for that lamb four times over, because he did such a thing and had no pity" (2 Samuel 12: 5-6 NIV).

Then Nathan said to David, "You are the man!" (2 Samuel 12: 7 NIV) *The prophet told David everything God recounted to him (2 Samuel 12:8-15).* Then David confessed, "I have sinned against the Lord." Nathan replied, "The Lord has taken away your sin; you shall not die" (2 Samuel 12:13 NIV).

David had been justifying in his mind why Uriah needed to die. He had not allowed himself to feel what Uriah or Bathsheba felt as he took control of their lives. There was such an imbalance of power and lack of compassion. David had lost, for maybe the first time in his life, the ability to empathize with someone else's pain.

So Nathan came with a story that God put together to break David's heart. For a few moments, hearing that story, David stopped being king. He was a shepherd boy again,

The Book on Bullies:
How to Handle Them without Becoming One of Them

rescuing his lambs from the mouths of lions and hungry bears. He was holding them on his lap along a grassy hillside and singing to them while he played his stringed instrument. He found his empathy and judged himself. Once, again, he became "a man after God's own heart" (1 Samuel 13:14 NIV).

That is what God wants for us and for our children. We can all fall into becoming bullies if we are not close to God and the purpose that he put into our hearts when he first called us by name. If we confess our sin and turn around, he will also put our sin away.

As parents, our job is to help our children heal hurts, including their own, and make amends where they can. The most significant discovery we can guide them to is finding their empathy and the God who first gave it to them.

The Road Back to Empathy

I want to rejoice in your victories,
Be sad when you have pain.
Caring how you feel, I will also heal,
I'll have found my compassion again.

Become Someone Who Won't Bully

My Own Personal Inventory

Have you ever bullied—even if you think it was unintentional?

Examples: (Check the boxes that apply)

☐ Belittled or demeaned someone
☐ Called someone derogatory names
☐ Insisted on trying to control someone
☐ Tried to hurt someone

What would you like to say or do if you could heal their hurt now?

Is it hard for you to say you are sorry? Why do you think that is so difficult?

Write out a short prayer. Ask God to forgive you and help you make changes in your behavior so you become a blessing.

Ask your family to pray for you and with you about being kinder.

My Plan of Action
to Become Someone Who Won't Bully

_____

_____

_____

_____

_____

_____

_____

_____

_____

_____

_____

_____

_____

_____

_____

_____

_____

_____

_____

_____

_____

_____

_____

CHAPTER 6

Be a Bystander No More

Bystander: *A person present but not involved; chance spectator; onlooker (*Dictionary.com).

We may have saved the best for last! I say this because "on the sideline" is where the majority of us are most of the time. If we are not the bully or being singled out by the bully, we could be in earshot or an eyewitness to bullying. Do we, however, notice when bullying is happening just a few steps away? If so, what impact does it have on us? Can we make a difference? Let's look at the research.

Adults often do not witness bullying despite their good intentions. Teachers intervene in only 14 percent of classroom bullying. They get involved in only 4 percent of bullying that happens outside the classroom.[1] Do students see others being bullied?

The Book on Bullies:
How to Handle Them without Becoming One of Them

Four out of five bullying instances at school are witnessed by other students. The witnesses join in three quarters of the time. This gives positive attention to the one doing the bullying. Although nine out of ten students say there is bullying in their school, adults rarely see bullying even if they are looking for it.[2]

Children who witness bullying are affected by what they see and hear. They are at risk for the use of tobacco, alcohol, or drugs. They have increased mental health problems such as depression and anxiety. They are even more likely to miss or skip school.[3]

Most teachers do their very best to teach while handling discipline problems in overcrowded classrooms. The good news is that as awareness is raised, everyone can take part in stopping abuses. School initiatives have reduced bullying by 15 to 50 percent. The most successful initiatives have involved the entire school community of teachers, staff, parents, students, and community members.[4]

Children can be afraid that if they report bullying, they will be the next victims. We can share with our children some hope. The research shows that children who report bullying to an adult are less likely to experience bullying in the future[5]

Parents want to know how to help their children be people who stand up for others, but they also don't want them in harm's way. One way is to give them a plan so they are ready if they see bullying taking place.

Tell them, "This is action you can take."

1. If you feel safe, stand next to the one being bullied and say, "Stop it!"
2. Find an adult and tell him or her what is happening.
3. Refuse to join in with the other kids who are watching.
4. Walk away (you take away attention the bully wants).
5. Offer to go with the person being bullied to tell a teacher or adult. [6]

Children I have worked with feel an inappropriate guilt over having witnessed bullying without trying to stop it. Even if the bullies were bigger, children will still carry the burden. Reassuring your children that it is not their fault will give them some relief. Explain that by telling you, they have helped someone and you will take it from there.

Parents can assist their kids in not being bystanders by recommending schools install suggestion boxes in all classrooms and school offices. Because these boxes will be somewhat protected in these rooms rather than in hallways, there is less likelihood other students will see what is written on the notes.

Most cities have hotlines where citizens can report crime anonymously. Why shouldn't our children have the same protection? If we want to stop bullying, we have to make it safe for the kids who see it to report it.

The most significant example our children and teenagers look for in life is the one we show them. Are we passive and apathetic when we see bullying or people being hurt? While we are watching others, our children are watching us.

The front page of the *Los Angeles Times*, November 4, 2011, ran this headline: "After Shocking Incidents Chinese Struggle To Instill Kindness." The news article reported the growing concern of the government of China over the lack of intervention by its citizens.

Cases were noted of children lying in the street bleeding as people walked around them. One report told of a mother begging people passing by to help get her child to the hospital. People refused to even stop. That child later died when help came too late. Officials were in the process of trying to decide how to motivate people to help one another. The passive, bystander problem is not only a national problem, it is a people problem.

Tim McGraw, the country singer, was giving a concert that I attended with my girlfriends. The concert was outside, and it was a beautiful evening. We all sang along, enjoying the fantastic music and Tim McGraw's performance on stage. Suddenly, to everyone's surprise, he stretched out his arm, pointing to a man sitting in one of the front rows center stage.

We heard through the sound system across the stadium, "You. Yes, you! You are out of here! I'm not kidding. Security, get this guy out of here or I'm not singing." His band was still playing when he ordered them off the platform and the stage went dark. After security did their job, Tim McGraw came back out and sat on the edge of the stage. The lights came back on and the only explanation he ever gave us was, "I am sorry. I won't stand by and watch a man treat a woman like that." Being the dignified therapist that I am, I jumped to my feet cheering, clapping, and yelling, "Yes!"

Later we talked one of the young security guys into finding out what security thought had happened. Supposedly, a drunken boyfriend had pushed his girlfriend down on the ground out of her chair. Whatever the case,

The Book on Bullies:
How to Handle Them without Becoming One of Them

the point is this: Tim McGraw refused to be a bystander. He said in effect, "No. Not on my watch."

An interesting aside is the fact that Tim's lovely wife and singer, Faith Hill, stood up for her husband in a similar fashion during one of their concerts together. A woman from the audience reached up to the edge of the stage and grabbed Tim McGraw in front of a crowd. Faith moved in front of her husband shouting to the woman, "Don't you ever touch him or grab him!"

Bullies beware: Tim and Faith will confront and they will not back down! Bystander must not be a word in their vocabulary. Faith and Tim, like Christ, intervened on behalf of others. Let's look at a few situations where the Lord Jesus stepped between the bullies and the bullied.

Jesus confronted corruption and robbery of the poor in temple life in Jerusalem. Animal sacrifices like lambs without blemish were brought into the temple for examination.

The moneychangers and dishonest religious officials found a clever method to extort money from people. They found any tiny flaw or defect on the animal and made the family buy a different animal from them—at an inflated cost, of course.

Then there were the moneychangers exchanging the Roman and Greek currencies. Only Jewish coins could be used for the half-shekel temple tax (Exodus 30:11-16) because the human portraits on pagan coins were considered idolatry. So the moneychangers provided the Tyrian (Jewish) coinage. Walvoord and Zuck, in *The Bible Knowledge Commentary,* tell us that there was no doubt fraud and extortion involved, even though only a small surcharge was legally permitted.[6]

The outer court of the temple was primarily a place for prayer by the devout Gentiles. This area, however, became a shortcut for people carrying their goods to get from one end of the city to another.[7]

The noise, arguing, and money changers shouting to get people to buy their animals must have been deafening. Who would be able to pray or even think of God in the middle of all that commerce?

More than once Jesus became angry over the way these thieves treated his Father's house of prayer and the poor. More than once in his ministry Jesus threw the moneychangers out, therefore cleansing the temple. He tipped over their tables. Coins flew everywhere and under the feet of the runaway animals so that no one knew which money was theirs!

Everyone knew this thievery had been going on and people had probably complained about it to the religious officials. Who would have ever stood up for God and for those in poverty trying to honor God with their sacrifices? Jesus did just that.

And he entered the temple and began to drive out those who sold, saying, "It is written, 'my house shall be a house of prayer' but you have made it a den of robbers" (Luke 19:45-46 RSV).

Jesus stood up publicly for many in the temple but sometimes he did it quietly and in private for individuals. He did this in Bethany where he sat down to eat with his friends and disciples. Martha served them and her brother Lazarus, whom Jesus had raised from the dead. Imagine how they all watched every bite the newly risen man chewed and swallowed.

Maybe no one noticed the other sister of Lazarus sitting by Jesus' side slowly holding his feet in her hands. She poured expensive perfumed oil over his ankles and feet and wiped it with her hair. Perhaps when the fragrance began to fill the room, the men finally looked over at Mary.

Judas smelled only money. He was the treasurer in charge of giving to the poor. He had been stealing from their small giving fund. So the bully who would eventually betray Jesus for thirty coins of silver began to badger Mary for her act of sacrificial love.

"Why was the ointment not sold for three hundred denarii and given to the poor?" This he said, not because

The Book on Bullies:
How to Handle Them without Becoming One of Them

he cared for the poor, but because he was a thief, and as he had the moneybox, he used to take what was in it. Jesus said, "Let her alone, let her keep it for the day of my burial. The poor you always have with you, but you do not always have me" (John 12: 4-8. RSV).

"Let her alone." Those simple words put Jesus between Judas and Mary. We could save someone from humiliation and ridicule with just those three words. Jesus even elevated her, commending her for understanding and taking to heart his words about his upcoming death. This concept was something his disciples had not yet allowed into their consciousness.

"Let her alone" was enough to stop the bullying. Adding the positive comment about her gave Mary back status and self-respect. This is a great gift to give someone in the presence of a bully and others. When we do this, we move from bystander to defender to advocate.

The last night Jesus stood between bullies and the people he loved was in the garden of Gethsemane. After Judas betrayed him with the identifying kiss, Jesus asked the soldiers to state who they wanted. When they named him he said, "I am he." Peter complicated things by drawing his sword and cutting off the ear of Malchus, the servant of the high priest. This put Peter and the other disciples in terrible danger.

The Book on Bullies:
How to Handle Them without Becoming One of Them

Then Jesus intervened to protect Malchus from Peter and prevent certain death for Peter by the soldiers. He touched and healed Malchus' ear to his head. The last protective act of Jesus; "I told you I am he, so if you seek me then let these men go" (John 18:8; Luke 22:51 RSV).

Jesus still runs interference for us. He answers prayer as our risen Savior at the right hand of his Father. We have someone who is our Lord but who also knows, first hand, what it feels like to walk around on this earth in a human body (Hebrews 4:15 NIV). 'For we do not have a high priest who is unable to sympathize with our weaknesses, but we have one who has been tempted in every way, just as we are, yet without sin.'

Jesus the Savior knows the weakness of the bullies, the bullied, and the bystanders. He died for us, and he lives so we can have empowered lives that glorify him every day.

We don't need to be afraid anymore.

Standing By

Lord, I thought you didn't care,
That you passively stood by.
Now, I know you were there,
Hearing my silent cry.

You care for the bullied
And for those who inflicted the pain.
You care for the bystander
Who never came.

You are still standing by,
Never far away from me.
Your Holy Spirit living in my life
Continues to make me free.

Be a Bystander No More

My Own Personal Inventory

What did you like about the way Jesus stood up for others?

Why don't we stop others when they pick on someone?
(Check the boxes you think are most true for you)

☐ I don't always notice someone is in trouble.
☐ I don't think it is any of my business.
☐ I am afraid the bully will turn on me.

Make a list of actions you can take or words you could say next time you see someone being bullied.

My Plan of Action
to Be a Bystander No More

_____

_____

_____

_____

_____

_____

_____

_____

_____

_____

_____

_____

_____

_____

_____

_____

_____

_____

_____

_____

_____

_____

_____

_____

_____

_____

_____

_____

_____

Notes

All website information cited was current as of October 24, 2011.

Chapter 4
Be Bully Proof

1. Dinkes, R.Kemp, J., and Baum K. (2009) (NCES 2009-022/NCJ226343) National Center for Education Statistics, Institute of Education Sciences, U.S. Department of Education and Bureau of Justice Statistics, Office of Justice Programs, U.S. Department of Justice, Washington, DC.

2. Devoy, J. F. and Kaffenberger, S. (2005) *Student Reports of Bullying: Results from 2001 School Crime Supplement to the National Crime Victimization Survey* (NCES 2005-310). U.S. Department of Education, National Center for Education Statistics, Washington, DC: U.S. Government Printing Office.

3. Department of Education website, www.ed.gov (The above cited information may be found on everychild.onevoice)

4. everydayhealth.com
   everydayhealth.com:http://everydayhealth.com/kids-health/0923/the-deadly-toll-of-bullying.aspx

5. everydayhealth.com
   http://www.everydayhealth.com/kids-health/0923/
   the-deadly-toll-of-bullying.aspx
6. stopbullying.gov
   http://www.stopbullying.gov/topics/effects/index.
   html
7. Stopbullying.gov
   http.//www.stopbullying.gov/young-adults/bully/
   index.html

Chapter 5
Become Someone Who Won't Bully

1. healthychildren
   http://www.healthychildren.org/English/ages-
   stages/toddler/pages/Aggressive-Behavior
2. stopbullying.gov
   http://www.stopbullying.gov/topics/effects/index.
   html
3. "Kindness: Changing Our World," Chuck Wall,
   Ph.D., Kindness, Inc., 2011.

Chapter 6
Be a Bystander No More

1. stopbullying.gov
   http://www.stopbullying.gov/topics/what_is_
   bullying/test_your_knowledge/index.html

2. stopbullying.gov
   http://www.stopbullying.gov/topics/what_is_
   bullying/test_your_knowledge/index.html
3. stopbullying.gov
   http://www.stopbullying.gov/topics/effects/index.
   html
4. stopbullying.gov
   http://www.stopbullying.gov/topics/what_is_
   bullying/test_your_knowlwdge/index.html
5. stopbullying.gov
   http://www.stopbullyin.gov/topics/what_is_
   bullying/test_your_knowledge/index.html
6. stopbullying.gov
   http://www.stopbullying.gov/teens/stand_against_
   bullying/index.html
7. *The Bible Knowledge Commentary* by Walvoord &
   Zuck, 254, Victor Books, 1983.
8. *The Bible Knowledge Commentary* by Walvoord &
   Zuck, 254, Victor Books, 1983.

Susan Boyd claims a dual citizenship
of
Bakersfield
and
Morro Bay, California.

Look for her upcoming books.

CPSIA information can be obtained at www.ICGtesting.com
Printed in the USA
BVOW082103300812

299269BV00001B/5/P